Dictionary of Silence

Aleš Debeljak

Translated from the Slovene by
Sonja Kravanja

With an Introduction by
Richard Jackson

Lumen Books
Santa Fe, New Mexico

Some of the translations in *Dictionary of Silence* have appeared in *Nimrod: International Journal of Prose and Poetry*, *Trafika: An International Literary Review*, *The Plumb Review*, and *Prisoners of Freedom: Contemporary Slovenian Poetry* (Pedernal). Permission to reprint these translations is gratefully acknowledged.

Support for the publication of this book was provided by The Trubar Foundation, Association of Slovenian Writers.

Lumen, Inc.
3900 Paseo del Sol
Santa Fe, New Mexico 87505
www.lumenbooks.org
Library of Congress Catalogue Number 99-67951
ISBN 0-930829-45-X
Printed in the United States of America
Slovar Tišine © 1987 Aleš Debeljak
Dictionary of Silence © 1999 Lumen, Inc.
Translation © 1999 Sonja Kravanja
Cover & book design: Dennis Dollens

for you

Introduction *9*

Biography of Dreamtime *13*

1

2

3

4

5

6

7

The Forms of Love *23*

1

2

3

4

5

6

7

Without Anesthesia *35*

1

2

3

4

5

6

7

Sketch of History *47*

1

2

3

4

5

6

7

Eye to Eye *57*

    1

    2

    3

    4

    5

    6

    7

Catalogue of Dust *69*

    1

    2

    3

    4

    5

    6

    7

Essay on Melancholy *79*

The World's Chronicle: The Poetry of Aleš Debeljak

Richard Jackson

"Between two worlds life hovers like a star," wrote Byron in Don Juan, and he goes on to show, in his ironic manner, that it is the task of the poet to explore the nature of this hovering. This notion goes back far, and in the modern age, Pascal's *Pensées* provides its basic paradigm. In Fragment 199, Pascal describes how we live in a world we can never know, trapped between a cosmos that is far too big to comprehend and a microscopic world too small to detail, a physical world whose laws escape us and an inner world that is equally puzzling. In our own time, this state manifests itself as what the philosopher Martin Heidegger calls "betweenness." Unable to understand either world, the poet makes metaphors, trying to explain one world in the terms of the other. Thus, metaphor becomes the basis of poetry, philosophy, of all essential thinking. Poetry becomes the essential way of creating history, world, thought, says Heidegger.

For Debeljak, who did graduate work in the social sciences at Syracuse University and who, like most central European poets, has been steeped in philosophy—he's written several critical books—such a habit of thinking is only natural. For example, the most famous locus of the "between" is perhaps Rilke's first Duino elegy (written in Italy, just a stone's throw from the Slovene border), one of the most philosophical poems of our age, in which the poet calls the angels down to try to intercede between man and the cosmos. Certainly, Rilke is a sort of poetic father for Debeljak, not only in subject matter, but also in his melancholy, elegiac tone. For both poets, the "between" is a fleeting moment that poet and poem try to expand:

. . . In people wandering restlessly
there always is some kind of map, stretching beyond the limits

of these lines. It borders the threshold of the unbearable. . . .
("Biography of Dreamtime 7")

The task of any elegy, after all, is to console, to provide a counter to what seems unbearable. That is the essential task

Debeljak's poetry sets for itself.

For Heidegger, the poet works in spasms, "moments of vision" (a phrase also used by Wordsworth and echoed by the acknowledged father of modern Slovene poetry Edvard Kocbek, a selection of whose poems, *Embers in the House of Night*, comprises the first volume in this Witter Bynner Translation Series), moments when the various tensions of the imagination are played out. So it is not surprising that this most philosophical of poets, Aleš Debeljak, finds himself, in Dictionary of Silence, in a world whose vocabulary is made up of words such as edge, border, moment, horizon, threshold, duration, and the corresponding vocabulary of the inner experiences othis state: wondering, desire, pain, longing, melancholy. For example, he says in "The Catalogue of Dust 2":

On the border between east and west a fox is barking into a sweetish night. Over a pillow some woman's hand is searching for kisses of times past. Time is ticking away in a wrist watch.

Not only the physical border, but a border between night and day (despair and hope?), sweetness and its opposite, the lost lover and the pillow cover, past and present, present and future, love and loneliness—all these borders go into defining the moment. In such a dialectical structure of oppositions, the simple ticking of a watch becomes an ironic statement about the absurdity of measuring time, however much it keeps marching against us: time is not a quantity but a quality, one made up of all the sensations that the poet restructures in the poem.

So the "between" is not the meeting point of some simplistic dialectic vision. As Heidegger says in *Being and Time*: "When such a moment makes the Situation authentically present, this making-present does not itself take the lead, but is held in that future which is in the process of having been. One's existence in the moment of vision temporalizes itself as something that has been stretched along in a way which is fatefully whole in the sense of an authentic historical constancy of the Self."[1] Here, even the future cannot be seen simply as future: it is held by the present, that is, by consciousness, by a structure of thinking, a metaphor; and the future itself never arrives, is always deferred—always a hope, a desire. In Debeljak's poetry, the structure of time, then, is amorphous, always being created within the poem itself:

Nothing points to the fact that this is but a simple glitter of
mirrors, repeating itself endlessly in the white china,
in the marble floors of foyers, in the gold-rimmed
glasses of atomic physicists: in them is reflected

a cruel gaze of a man who nobody knows. Who steps effortlessly
from the past into the present.
("Eye to Eye 3")

    Here, time becomes a space to wander around in: the man becomes like the memorials referred to in the next few lines, the space we live in one where his face "freezes for a second," yet where we experience time, then, as "an infinite elegy." For all the elegiacs here, the poetry is one of celebration, a poetry filled with sudden leaps, with shifts between the cosmic and the everyday, the sensual and the ideal: it is poetry, that is, which is first of all filled with life.
    The terror then becomes like what Shelley recorded in his poem "Mont Blanc," where he traces an imagined journey up the side of the mountain only to wonder at the top, unseen for the clouds, if all were not simply emptiness. Is there, in a scene, anything beyond us, Shelley asks. As Debeljak's "The Catalogue of Dust 4" expresses it, in a more assertively negative mode: "The frame of the extinct sky is empty, emptier than empty." The poet next populates that world, first with images of winter—emptiness, bones, glass—, images of sterility, and then, by associating some of these images with deer—their warm bodies, how they populate the forests of America,—he ends with a transcendent image in which the moment and the small space expand: "Just think how some foreign/ bird sharply cuts the air above the Mojave desert."
    Still, even though the poet is able to create such worlds, even though the outside cosmos might appear to grow a bit more benign, the inner self, the inner world threatens. In "Eye to Eye 4," for example, Debeljak describes a scene like that in a Dutch floral painting, then turns suddenly to the poet: "And inside the one who/ writes these verses a strange pain." In a few moments, the inner worlds of all creatures witness

"the unbearable force of duration." When the inner world is again made right, the outer threatens once again: it is an endless task for the poet. It is a dialectic of inner and outer, vision and chaos, hope and despair, which the poetry is always confronting, mending, holding off against the darkness.

For Debeljak, part of the sense of constancy that Heidegger mentions comes from the very form of the verses: regular, in four-line stanzas, three stanzas to a poem, seven poems to a sequence (except for the last, which has but one), seven sequences to the book. Within this format, the poet manipulates the vision so that one might have, for instance, a stanza where one idea is extended throughout, a following stanza where several ideas are densely packed. The result is a varied pace, a complex rhythm capable of dealing with dialectics of this ever-changing world. Such, then, is mature poetry in a first book of poems by a poet whose unique music and vision offer a way to experience the edges of our lives as the centers, a poetry that makes of those dangerous edges a world provisionally comprehensible, always in the process of being created anew.

---

[1]Martin Heidegger. *Being and Time*. Translated by John Macquarrie and Edward Robinson. New York: Harper & Row, 1962.

BIOGRAPHY OF DREAMTIME

BIOGRAPHY OF DREAMTIME 1

The shadows thickening, the long backs of mountains sinking
into the ocean waves. The voice of a trumpet, a lonely sound.
Perhaps coming from a radio. —Somewhere on the edge of
the visible world the hidden power of never-ending blues

is sinking in the quicksand of Magreb hills. —
The metal sound of a midday bell. Veterans, asleep in wicker
rocking chairs. The soft leather of their boots smells of pitch
and vindictive battalions. —In the burned grass of the garden

lies ripe fruit. The white walls of small houses shimmer in the heat,
the officers' livers are corroded by lethargy. Which transforms
them into a catalogue of plants. —One of them at times speaks
verses from Dante. Many deaths are quietly gathering in him.

BIOGRAPHY OF DREAMTIME 2

The hands of wall clocks have been still for ages. The deer's children
have hardened into a lithograph. — More of a description follows:
boiled fruit strides into the head: in the weightless dizziness
an apparition. Which multiplies encounters with a theory of poison.

Many a time. It is not surprising: the recollection is melting
like wax. The magnetic spell of crime is now stronger than the
force of gravitation. Not unusual. As when in dreams doves flutter
away, the memory of them lost in an instant. — The moment when

the atmosphere trembles with wavelengths: luring in the memory of forlorn
places, of various crimes, of symmetry of slow dying through the layers
of time. — All of these. — With a green snake's head a human trace is
tattooed, glowing with the desire to break through the sound barrier.

BIOGRAPHY OF DREAMTIME 3

This poem is for you, the nameless. Who, irritated and weary from
monotonous waiting for who knows what, are still wandering
through time. Not writing a journal. No body like you writes one.
You are on your own. Left alone in your longing for the future. Surviving

the refugee camps, biding farewell to the ornamental style of
Secession architecture with ease. Perhaps you'll glance at an elusive
glitter of arms in the feathers of titmice. Hear your solitary whistle.
That lasts. That stretches far. Until it hardens into an elegy.

Nothing you can do. That's the way it has to happen. Then despair,
gently rustling inside us. That's just it. You may drink another
six bottles, but your physique will not come to life in the mirror
of a stranger's memory. Until the end you'll be the only one. Alone.

BIOGRAPHY OF DREAMTIME 4

Banks, banners, ships, holidays, cock fights, epaulets,
copper-plate engravings of English horses, dead sentinels
and elite divisions. All this comes and goes. It disappears
like chatter in some quick nap in the afternoon.

Come to terms with it. The arrival and the deserted scene are
one and the same. Instead of the planted tree and pages of
the testament, only a name somebody writes down in a dictionary remains.
Nothing more. Oh, someone will perhaps remember for an instant the

metamorphosis from paleness to scarlet: as it sometimes happens with
kings. Besides that, truly nothing. — Tear the crumpled carnation
off your chest, bend toward the geometry of granite squares, and
breathe your last breath. Now. Like those in Stammenheim prison.

BIOGRAPHY OF DREAMTIME 5

On the border between lips and tongue someone counts off
the days left to a devastating earthquake that Halley's comet did
not predict. And bird hunters gather full traps, and family
houses are sinking into slime. As if from far away grape leaves,

burned with Peronospora, were falling gently on the house fronts.
And the spears of the white hunters find unerringly the softness
of loins and stomach: I'd like to put down the final period.
I feel the rhetorical figure of eternity does not exist.

Behind the closed window a stretched sound is announcing the tide
of sadness, rippling stealthily inside exhausted people. The thick
fog evens up, the room grows wider. Under the railroad embankment
a couple is getting lost in a slow lovemaking.

BIOGRAPHY OF DREAMTIME 6

To survive everything that persists in apparent harmony.
To be snow in a warm hand that freezes from the weight
of the silvery crystals. To be a letter in Sanskrit. Buckwheat
honey. To be less than the lust for infinity and classified

documents. To become a poppy blossom, a tobacco leaf, a barren
landscape. A word that nobody will ever be able to correctly repeat.
To whisper like a rhyme from a sonnet and to sink at once into
chaos. To be the senseless clamor of the birds, echoing in all

the places as the one and only tune. To be endless fields,
blues in the memory of forty-year-olds. To survive the anguish
of the place, narrowing like the pupil of an animal. That
attacks with horrifying power, settling its overdue debt.

BIOGRAPHY OF DREAMTIME 7

Beneath the horizon of humid tropics things could have been different.
Perhaps his neighbors would let him stay in his room for at least
three days. Let the leaden air lie on his eyes, staring widely at
the hunt and the escape. And the homesickness that none of them ever

gets rid of. So that the deadly crisp song could sound in his
ear. And the indifferent buzzing of bee swarms would close in
the circle. But I don't believe it. In people wandering restlessly
there always is some kind of map, stretching beyond the limits

of these lines. It borders the threshold of the unbearable. And
the premonition of the dull cuckoo singing breathes clearly in them.
In their liver a raw force burns painfully. When close to a woman
it changes into longing. The smell of cinnamon goes with it.

FORMS OF LOVE

And I'm here to stay with you
And no matter what you do
When you're lonely—I'll be lonely too

Yazoo, *You and Me Both*

FORMS OF LOVE   1

This is the place. Small animals jump frightened into the murky forest, even farther—into an almost erased chronicle from long-gone times. Many years later my son will discover it, bewildered. — A late hour chimes in softened thoughts,

in the stomach rumble liters of anise liquor. —This is the place. When I was arriving it looked like a storm. The rain is unleashed now. I feel how the words are stretching irrepressibly beyond me. I wish to say nothing. — Perhaps the time for winter freeze is

coming. I haven't finished yet: I incessantly listen to the blood, circulating in my veins. I share with you the fear of voices from the dark. I am leached by a shudder. Oh to know and to forget that all you need to die is carbon monoxide. Quiet now. Be somebody else.

FORMS OF LOVE 2

For Malcolm Lowry

This night he'll be oblivious to bay harbors and weak
comparisons. He'll lie down with a woman he—how very
simple—does not want to wipe from his memory. It
will make him very vulnerable. Under the windows people will

gather slowly, singing in a drawl. This is better than talking.
Someone will perhaps drink tequila. The sky circle will now expand
the volume of the lovers' brief dreamtime. Meanwhile not much
will happen. He'll breathe softly his forever into her neck. The

fluttering of wings at four a.m. will be only an illusion. And
before the neighboring street becomes aglow with dawn, she'll
know the metaphor of love is made of metal. Like the clasp on a safety
belt. They border on each other. Silent now. And forever.

FORMS OF LOVE 3

You are weary. Your gaze is feeling out things. Quiet breathing
of smokers is heard and mirrors are still. You don't know
anyone. It could be worse. All you need is a low chair and the shape
of a woman's head in the damp stain on the wallpaper. You are not

afraid. You will never return again to be a reader of short poems,
an interpreter of sonnets. You will die without being able to
exhaust all the forms of reality. You won't regret that. You are
not pretending, the art of wandering is no longer alien to you.

In rooms, plains, and the sky, a smell of turpentine. What rustles
under your restless hands is not the paper of this poem. You
will persevere in the cracks of time, contemplating the surface
of the sea you have sailed across so many a time.

FORMS OF LOVE 4

Subdued desire makes him sad. The light forks low over
the frozen earth: he woke up in his dream and strode barefoot
into the image of another man. Under his fingers, like
the spring snow, large biographies are thawing. Perhaps

he will now be forgotten by all, as he had wished a thousand
times. As a wide lynx path in the deep forest of Mt. Snežnik.
And full of viper-bite marks and restlessness,
shut into the harmony of odd pleasure and absence:

I don't know what he is thinking when he contemplates the quail's
eggs. When he gazes at the line in the horizon and the alloy of
distances. He is blind, perhaps. After all, he is not telling the things
others can tell. It seems to me he may be running out of words.

FORMS OF LOVE 5

On your last journey you haven't discovered anything. In the early morning after you returned: a flash of recollection about the Jewish quarter, about the kiss. The woman's shadow will remain, that is true. And Venice, a delusive game of echoes, always a bit too

plentiful. — You've already lost your way. In the emptiness of your stomach a dark flower is growing. — Which is disappearing in insanity like water in water. There is no other life, that much is clear now. A trip is over, but the tension in the thighs and the skull's

base does not go away. — You are utterly unnoticed. In short, nobody. With the shape of an animal before it vanishes into dusk. Only its eye at times flashes toward the sky. — On the street the voices of children at play. Distant. They are not here. Silence. And the light in your room.

FORMS OF LOVE 6

Listen, she said. Listen to the deadly silent labor in which I'll
give birth to something that transcends me. Get ready for the south
wind, the one that makes people sick, get ready for the faceless
noise of passion, love, demanding poems, sins. You'll come to

understand: without me you will never enter the anthology of
light. If you didn't meet me, you didn't meet anybody
else. Perhaps this takes your breath away. But: does it change
a thing? I describe you with warmth in my voice, even

when whispering. Because you pulsate with my heartbeat.
Because my smile runs down your veins. And the image you'll
take across the ocean will be filled with me. What transcends
me is the two of us, our moss, silver, vulnerability, a long long journey.

FORMS OF LOVE 7

For Boštjan Seliškar, again

Nothing is attainable. No voice is ever doubled.
As if it had never happened. Things move on, orderly.
In the morning the sun will rise again. Blood runs through the veins.
You are nothing. For everybody else but one woman, you are

a deep darkness on the river bottom. A hopelessly smooth stone
with a bluish tint. A niche in the well. A nobody's beginning,
that no one recognizes. Like Scott's diary, buried under
the polar storm. You are nothing. Perhaps you are my sadness,

broad as the sky. And the space and the emptiness of a film,
forever rolled in the reel. The town is now no less helpless
than it was before. Only I—I can add this—will be vibrating at
the frequency of your silence, waiting for you to answer.

WITHOUT ANESTHESIA

*Naked I stand, alone, without
a heart. Without the center of the world.
My tears don't wash away a thing.
Salt corrodes the aroused skin.*

Brane Bitenc, *I See You Leaving*

WITHOUT ANESTHESIA 1

Things are empty. There is nothing in them. As if they were the fruit of some failed plan. A landscape lies in the water, growing green from some kind of plant. Overshadowed by the lines of the horizon. Filled with emptiness everybody is afraid of.

This morning perhaps does smell of jasmine tea. But this is not to say it has any meaning. You may keep taking walks along the shore, it doesn't make a difference. What your look scoops up is no more than a bitter apparition. It reminds you of the images

of all happenings, already known to you. You refuse to find the space for things. That last longer than your imagination, your hope, your secrets. You are encircled by things. This actually isn't all that bad. Only they are reliable. They are.

WITHOUT ANESTHESIA 2

Helpless as a plain that never sinks into
the horizon, now even more so: as water in the lake,
for example, agitated by a nightfall, that cannot
overflow the banks. Helpless you are longing

for death, waiting, watching, breathing imperceptibly.
But so what? The expected image does not appear in the shoal.
Not even for a second, or less. Sight and hearing are of
no use: under the undulating water's surface there is no more

depth than you found in a serene gesture of a pregnant woman
you saw one morning on your street. The force of gravitation
tells you so. And the names, days and nights, the lives
of foreign generations. They are all useless.

WITHOUT ANESTHESIA 3

It is time. Speak of what has already been
said before. To avoid misunderstanding. Start
wherever you wish. You won't suffer more than you suffer
now. The bird's taking off from the water's surface already

announces the fall. You won't lose anything either. As much
as you have given, that much is yours. I understand that
in fleeing into a foreign language you long for silence. That
doesn't tear your body apart, since you know it from within.

For only people die, not their silence.
The flock of starlings, though, flying home, is noisy.
You will need to raise your voice. Speak now!
Tell. How quiet you are, becoming the breath of all the people.

WITHOUT ANESTHESIA 4

Enough talking. I'd rather fall asleep. Above me a flight
of wild geese, inside me a dry cough and embers. —
A gust of wind turns a weather vane. At the end
only I am left. It is about time I become

the acoustics of silence, the unspoken parallel dialogue.
I won't be anybody's scream anymore, crystallized in the core
of amber. Stars are cold, people are turning on lights in their
houses. The ultrasound of night strides the world. What else

can I expect, what else can I give? I've memorized the rhythm
of the physical pain the world starts with every day. I know
the illusions of images and ancient manuscripts. I'd like to be
alone again. Like the weeping of a baby, abandoned by his mother.

WITHOUT ANESTHESIA 5

Permeated by a shudder, by despair: every thing in your room,
or anywhere else, every thing has its name. Dizziness fills
up your days, you sit still as you watch
the blurred TV screen, empty courtyards,

book and record covers, narrow stairways: the starless sky
is repeating this despair on thin ice, stretched bluishly
over some puddle. Useless cloud shapes,
how little love! With your lips, much shyer than you

think, you glide haltingly over the immobility of things.
The pulse of blood does not disturb the silence, only you still suffer.
Like your pain, you don't want to be who you are: things endure
without you. For them you already are as dead as a trampled rose.

WITHOUT ANESTHESIA 6

Distance trying to appear
Something more than obstinate

Elizabeth Bishop, "Argument"

A heavy, perceptible quivering of air, fields of mimosa,
the distinctive smell of some root, the glow of a lamp she
holds up in her hand: what noise does she hear around
her head, now half immersed in the evening mist?

A cold sweat runs down her brow, gathering in her
wide-open eyes. The salty liquid burns her. Her gaze darkens.
The silence is growing. Fire from dry grasses starts burning
under her feet. In a moment she will have to forget the happy days.

On her lips even you won't distinguish the parched impression
of pain collecting in her. The earth keeps on rotating,
perhaps nothing happened. The forest is silent, forked
paths ahead. Standing quietly she listens to the sound of emptiness.

WITHOUT ANESTHESIA 7

Wet asphalt. And the serene, eternal flow of minerals in the mountain
and valley. Unknown to you, indifferently quiet, like lichens
in the forest of faraway northern landscapes. An everyday phrase
from a conversation, that lasts forever. And consists of four,

five words. Outcried, perhaps, only by a love song. —
The phosphoric dial on a watch glows. The date of your helplessness.
You sensed a long time ago there is no adequate translation
for it. — If you'd invent a language without verbs, then,

perhaps, you'd live longer. You'd deliver all the weight of
the passing of time into a touch, never expressed. The skull will
thus be boiling, and other places too. The face will petrify.
In the retina will remain, like a blind spot, Moby Dick.

SKETCH OF HISTORY

SKETCH OF HISTORY 1

In the narrow shadows of houses lie dogs. Bramble and
ivy climb up the chilly walls.
A movie theater features *Maria's Lovers*.
Someone drinks his eighth beer in a damp one-room

apartment. Thunderbolts are hitting his
body. He doesn't hear the flutter of swallows
already late for their flight south. Sharp as an
oyster edge the longing for the white whale cuts

through his brain. Through his bone and skin. He'll repeat
the old story. In his quivering muscles a fiery liquid
is gathering. In his head insane birds and insects
scream. In his forever-wounded eyes glitters the ocean.

SKETCH OF HISTORY 2

Let nobody cry, let nobody silence his trepidation:
for a short while let words and things disappear. It snows
over Sicily. — Hold your breath. Let only the disintegration
of silence stay, transient as night damp on the windows of a labyrinth.

There should be no sadness. — So what, if the blood drips. Your
IDs smell after it. But no. Do not say a word. — Let there be a tunnel
only where echoes multiply. Let your silence chime inaudibly. Because
there will be no more solid ground under you. In your skull

you will carry the image of a void, sharp like a glance through a train
window. You will never again sink your head in pillows. On the
surface of your skin there will be cuts, traces of bites and acid.
Unperceived you will have one thought only: Let me vanish, too.

SKETCH OF HISTORY 3

The children have fallen asleep a long time ago. It seems, for
a moment, the modest number of days they've lived here means
no more than ashes from some hunting story. You named
the rest with love, but to one of them you assigned

boats, travels, used books, and an epitaph,
put together clumsily. He will know more proverbs than
silver coins, he will be cruel to domestic animals, one night
he will, in a place you'll be longing to reach till your death day,

kill a man. He won't lose the ecstasy of madness, he will be
a solitary, longing in unbearable pain to be less than his fame.
He will like to move in the dark, murmuring about the danger
and the singing of a bird, freezing tonight on his window sill.

SKETCH OF HISTORY 4

Your eyes are itching from the tepid air of the closed place.
The mountain peak is still covered with snow. Slowly the window
panes mist over. You are getting up, drenched by ordinary rain,
cold penetrating your veins and bones. The ravaged plain looks

like a side on the east of paradise. A silent fiddler from
another poem consistently plays the same tune, his back leaning
against a tree. From the wall poster a sharp profile of an
unknown woman stares down at you. — The tissue in your skull boils

from a salty longing to understand the language of poisonous herbs. —
Hope drips into your mouth and heart. — You hardly move, stricken by
a lack of words: a second, perhaps less, before dawn floods the
wolfish world, you will grow immensely and faint from desire.

SKETCH OF HISTORY 5

Here is just the same as there. No difference. When dying,
everybody is the universe. A hollowed dream, in which the name
is lost. Drawers in the bedroom hang open. The feet of pensive
friends are sinking into the powdery snow. It seems to me that from

the last signature on the letter, written just before death, a pelican
is rising. His white wings overshadow the sky. Unless this is simply
a reflection of indifference in the eyes of men, leaning over the dead
body. I could be silent, not saying a thing. I could be ashes in the

urn the people closest to him carefully carry home. But: with every
single death die all the things. Which I won't itemize,
since everybody knows of them. I will finish this poem. After it
a cloud is left, a gust of wind, nothingness.

SKETCH OF HISTORY   6

In the morning, when each of us has less sugar in the blood.
In the morning, when the whiteness of day stains the window.
In the morning, when dreamtime reaches its zenith. And is
close to flux. The despair from our dream's cinder is exhausting us.

My morning is not simpler. I am again flesh and blood. — Steam is
rising from blankets. The wake-up time is defined already, well
beforehand. Like everything else that has happened today. Arteries
are filling up. The field of vision trembles with expectation.

I won't mention any symbols. These are not an issue here.
It is time to keep quiet about things that count. That are warm from touching:
here, there, beyond. That shine colder than stars, impressed into the
brain. That don't fade like a footstep from a dead era, or this verse.

SKETCH OF HISTORY   7

The same nightmare, the same addiction to alcohol, the same
waiting for the eternal elsewhere: that finally fulfills itself
in the same slimy solution. Like a poorly made etching.
The scorpion's poison, engraved in it, doesn't spill over

its frame. But blends at times with the lymph-like fluid
of someone who feels the white sadness of the world. That is
stretched out in the windless landscape. That endures. Like
a dolphin on its circular path through the seas. The bottom of

sharpened senses burns with bitterness, tears, fleeing. It makes
everybody huddle on the edge of the night like frightened deer.
It makes everybody close their eyes: it doesn't help, though. —
After the seventh day the game crumbles into scenes from everyday life.

EYE TO EYE

Laissez les fauvettes de mai
Pour ceux qu'au fond du bois enchaîne,
Dan l'herbe d'où l'on ne peut fuir,
La défaite sans avenir.

Arthur Rimbaud, "Les Corbeaux"

EYE TO EYE 1

Somewhere ahead of him, quite far ahead, perhaps above a barren
field: a distinctive sound. Lingering in the air like the chirping of
swallows. Dangerously sharp sound. He hears it as clearly as the high C
of Ella Fitzgerald. It can break a glass if it catches the right

resonance. His lips are moist, his stomach cramping. That much is
clear. He listens feverishly, thinking of the dreamers who never
awake in the circles of day and night. They are driven by unknown
passion, effortlessly entering cathedral walls, lives of poets, pure

facts, Plato's dialogues and old city quarters of Marakesh. Left
alone, forever. Like a bush, blossoming in the dead of the winter, which
disappears in the spring without a trace. In this poem they are a tone
in the sharp sound, a soft chiming of a gong, an appearance and nothing.

EYE TO EYE 2

In which dimly-lit city quarter, famous for its movie theaters —
in which cheap night shelter will he, growing thinner
every day, with an invisible flower of insanity in his eyes,
die alone? The volume of his aimless travels will be measured precisely,

as will his sympathies for the soldiers from the Spanish Civil War.
No more than sympathies. He will know of many monotonous comparisons
I am making up right now. He won't be using them to silence
the nameless pain, glowing in his intestines. A corrosive blotch

sinks its roots into his veins. Now nobody means anything to anybody.
No force can keep him in place, he'll only pause long enough to wipe his
sweating forehead. Under the sky of a strange world even a tremor
of frozen tones—Laurie Anderson, perhaps—does not hold him back.

EYE TO EYE 3

Nothing points to the fact that this is but a simple glitter of
mirrors, repeating itself endlessly in the white china,
in the marble floors of foyers, in the gold-rimmed
glasses of atomic physicists: in them is reflected

a cruel gaze of a man who nobody knows. Who steps effortlessly
from the past into the present. His violence is carved into the multitude
of war memorials, forever translated into all the languages
spoken in the world. —There must be, then, a light angle under

which his face freezes for a second. So that every child memorizes
it. In the floating dusk inside apartments it changes into
an infinite elegy, that doesn't heal any wounds. No, it opens more.
It is whispered in every corner of the hemisphere.

EYE TO EYE 4

You are watching: you carry him inside your heart. You are hurting
with longing. A shape of a cloud reminds you of him time and again.
He is on your mind when you drift out of the room into
the courtyard, carelessly talking about hunting the game.

You believe, for an instant, you've seen him in the death agony
of all the people who have journeyed through you in vain. You
watch him in the feathers of Brazilian parrots, in the black algae
in the sewer, in the thunder of October. You watch him.

You don't see him. He is lost for you as a naked woman in the smoke
of an opium pipe. But this is not betrayal. He leaves, he
comes, he is gone. Like a blurred trace of a silver sea gull,
traveling through time. He is simply gone. Your sigh is useless.

EYE TO EYE 5

Above the wet roof of an ossuary insects are gathering in
a purple dawn. Like a bad imitation of an eighteenth-century
Dutch painting. Strollers halt their steps. Nothing happens.
Perhaps this is but nature morte. And inside the one who

writes these verses a strange pain. In its chronicle the constellations
thaw. And the hidden gentleness. That was pushed away, blended
with the gun powder. So that those who have killed are once
again becoming fearful. Nobody knows them.

They are the fruit and the seed of another world. With
the ice-cold gaze they stare into the night that is less
terrifying than themselves, whispering of emptiness inside
their bodies. About the unbearable force of duration.

EYE TO EYE 6

For a long time he hasn't gone anywhere. Hasn't changed his
observation spots or lit his menthol cigarettes. He hasn't been
born again in the forceful foreign verbs, the membrane of his
earlobe hasn't trembled differently, he hasn't slept with black women.

Every month is now cruel for him, not only April. Like an empty street,
leading to the opposite direction. He is oblivious to the phone
ringing. He is afraid he'll miss the falling of star dust, dispersing
above him, somewhere condensing into a miraculous mute poem.

It sometimes seems to him he already sees this somewhere. He doesn't
care about city alleys, filled with delivery boys, linen shirts,
buses, rattling of glass. Immovable and quiet he stares at the 200
watt bulb. In its monotonous flickering he sees the outline of the world.

EYE TO EYE 7

There is no time yet to forget that piercing scream, impossible
to imitate. It pulsates on the wavelengths of memory. As if it were
all about the love song of a woodcock. Pure and clear. — Even when you
smoke at night on the veranda, this image still makes you shiver

slightly. It has no negative, and glitters dimly like a blade of
a soldier's dagger. Which has not yet been displaced by some literary
trick. You certainly could move away, change your IDs, become
a granite crystal. —You could. But you won't.—Only when you

know how to arrange the mirrors in order, only then you'll become
yourself. You'll see the odyssean history. Beyond the hell, beyond
the paradise. Naked you'll feel each trepidation of planets. A carnivorous
flower will grow within your spine. One, and changing every day.

CATALOGUE OF DUST

CATALOGUE OF DUST 1

Over the leaf of thin paper runs a crack. A weather vane turns
gently in the eternal circle of the day; everything ever written
is already evaporating in four directions. — He, who now watches
the marsh blossom, sees the seed and decanting of juices. Sees

everywhere the shore and the sea that might not exist. In his eyes
the suburbs of New Orleans grow red. Sees somebody, who was poisoned
to his bones by sadness. He will, on the dusty surface of a wine
glass, watch with melancholy a pale silhouette. Distinguishing it

from anxiety and violence, from the song of a nightingale, from
parchment meditations, from selfishness and impatience. He won't return
what he hasn't taken. He will measure love and the volume of eternity. —
He, who watches now, sees a woman with a dark spot in the softness of her back.

CATALOGUE OF DUST 2

It appears like a smooth marten fur, leaping from the undergrowth
into an anguished omen. No muffled thundering of horned owls can be
heard. Things go into hiding, evermore. A bitter juice from
snake-grass deepens the wound as it runs over it.

On the border between east and west a fox is barking into a sweetish
night. Over a pillow some woman's hand is searching for kisses of
times past. Time is ticking away in a wrist watch. The atmosphere
is bleeding from all the above. As if this image would depend

on somebody who is also frightened. Spellbound people watch
intently how a straight line shoots up from the east side,
penetrating bread, almond seeds and cornea.
This, too, has been written down before.

CATALOGUE OF DUST 3

Today will not be different from other days. He will nurse
his boredom and renew the botany from the brief afternoon dreams.
He will stand by the window curtain, longer than usual. He will
open the shutters, look toward the town squares, the streets,

and into a May dusk. In the dust of a garden he will, for an instant
or two, see a stag. Stalked by a soldier. The temperature in his
brain will rise, behind his back he'll probably hear a saxophone
player practicing for a gig. As if by a coincidence a shiver will run

down his spine. He'll feel the taste of cheap rum in his throat.
He'd like to believe everything is behind him. As if possessed by
the pounding of monsoon rains and moaning of paratroopers
somebody tall and black will rise from the collective memory.

CATALOGUE OF DUST 4

The frame of the extinct sky is empty, emptier than empty. No starlings or any other birds. No cloudy weavings, no long sleepless walks in January. Perhaps there is a south breeze, but this is not important. White frost crackles under somebody's feet. You are at peace, hollowed

to the nerve's end. You are without hatred or envy, you don't care about the calendar of people in your life. Bare fish bone. — I could keep talking about your dislike of closed spaces. — You are smooth as Venetian glass. Silent and dense like water. Water, water. —

Deer are freezing in the forest. Their warm skin, how it breathes with the concentric circles of dusk! A name, a body, a glance: impregnated with the American plain. Just think how some foreign bird sharply cuts the air above the Mojave desert.

CATALOGIE OF DUST 5

Honey is dripping from a wild cherry tree. It used to heal wounds.
Not any longer. — Disappointment grows in somebody's lungs.
Facts follow each other. Not changing anything, of course.
Nor astronomy or tools for anesthesia: nothing is interesting

or exciting anymore. — Afterward it rained, most likely. —
And he says quietly: I'll disintegrate from stillness.
His widened nostrils aren't catching the smell of ozone and
hatred anymore. Hatred which for everybody else will forever

linger like mists above the melancholic riverbed of the Danube.
An early blooming of a dandelion, yellowing dully in his hands.
And long fields of shamrock, stretched as bodies of war victims.
He will now look around. Whispering inaudibly gracias a la vida.

CATALOGUE OF DUST 6

Then there was whispering in the next-door room. And quiet moaning of the wooden floor. If you'd glance through the window in this very moment, you'd see a bus on the narrow empty road. The vein in your throat would be throbbing faster. Your mouth would be slightly open.

You grew up on the street. The whole world is now asleep. Children and history as well. Nobody thinks of flying. The volume of memory is hardening, faces turned toward the wall. Perhaps, in your dreams, they are being taken to be shot. The next day you dream about a live woman.

Her nude body, etc., etc. You never sing. You could, sometimes at night, stride into a park and whistle softly. Then you'd perhaps notice the shapes, the sounds, the colors of dreamtime where you would not die. Over and over again.

CATALOGUE OF DUST 7

The seam in the sky has vanished. The land has sunk in the water.
If there will once be an urgent need to return, there will be no
path left. Into the dark edge of the horizon a warship is framed,
sailing through soldiers' dreams. No person around. No one to ask

about the squeaking of mice, trembling in the air. No one to wonder
why flies are gathering into a swarm. Perhaps this is history for
them. For those who dream all this. Let the flowers wither, buckwheat,
linden-tree leaf. Because this morning even the animals don't

rise from their cold shelters. One more sign of fear. Somewhere
above the Hungarian plain sings a nightingale. I think not for long.
A gun-blast will take him out of the image. Once and forever.
As if made of pure carbon seems this dreaming, the heritage of no one.

Neca Falk

Born in Ljubljana, Slovenia in 1961, the poet, editor, translator, and professor **Aleš Debeljak** graduated in comparative literature from the University of Ljubljana and later received his Ph.D. in Social Thought at Syracuse University, New York. He was a Senior Fulbright fellow at the University of California, Berkeley and a fellow at the Institute of Advanced Study in Budapest.

A leading Central European poet, Debeljak has published five books of poems and eight books of essays in his native Slovenian. His books in English translation include *Anxious Moments* as well as *Dictionary of Silence* and *The City and the Child*, published in 1999 by Lumen Books, Santa Fe, and White Pine Press, Buffalo, respectively.

Debeljak's volume of personal and analytical meditation, *Twilight of the Idols: Recollections of a Lost Yugoslavia*, has been translated into twelve languages. Other of his works have appeared in Japanese, German, Croatian, Polish, Hungarian, Czech, Slovak, and Italian translations. He won the Slovenian National Book Award and the Miriam Lindberg Israel Poetry for Peace Prize.

Debeljak edited *Prisoners of Freedom: Contemporary Slovenian Poetry* as well as sections for *Shifting Borders: East European Poetries in the Eighties*. Recently, he edited a comprehensive anthology, *The Imagination of Terra Incognita: Slovenian Writing 1945-1995* and published a scholarly study, *Reluctant Modernity: The Institution of Art and its Historical Forms*. In addition to translating the *Selected Poems of John Ashbery* into Slovenian, he has edited an anthology of American metafictional writing and published a collection of essays on American literature.

Debeljak chairs the Department of Cultural Studies at the University of Ljubljana in the Slovene capital, where he and his American wife, Erica Johnson, live with their three young children.

ESSAY ON MELANCHOLY

No rain was falling. It probably wasn't snow, either. For some hours already, for all my life, I am disappearing into the text. I don't talk to others, because I don't even talk to myself. I am vanishing into the text to bring the poetics of this hallucination to light. There is no other way. I wonder why people read the documents of this cleansing. I have no more words left. Even these are not necessary. Hi ho.

July 1986